God's Calling and the Authority of the Believer

Equipping Christian leaders and intercessors to discern God's calling in their lives and assert the authority of their calling as forceful men and women by praying Kingdom prayers through the themes of John.

by Clyde J Hodson

All rights reserved. No part of this book may be reproduced in any form without permission in writing from the author, except in the case of brief quotations embodied in critical articles or reviews.

All scripture quotations are taken from the Holy Bible: New International Version (NIV)

Copyright © 2011 by Clyde Hodson

All rights reserved

ISBN-13:978-1720395072

ISBN-10: 1720395071

I want to thank Becky Scheffrahn, Jeanine Smith, and Carolyn Trimmer for reading through this material and giving very valuable input to its final product. To Carol Harris for her work in the coordination and editing of this publication. Special thanks are in order to Jack Jackson, Beth Marshall, and Larry Yandell for encouragement and contribution to the editing and proofing of this booklet. I am grateful to my wife, Mary Lynne, and my daughters, Kara, Lindsay and Meagan who have patiently allowed me to seek the Lord in prayer in the early hours of the morning and come to a place of abiding in Him.

For more information about this ministry, please contact:

*Prayer*Mentor

Clyde Hodson

PO Box 13856

Arlington, TX 76094

www.prayermentor.org

clydehodson@prayermentor.org

Table of Contents

Introduction — 11

John the Baptist's Perspective Towards Ministry — 12

A Child of the Flesh — 13

Jesus The Sovereign Lord — 15

The Priestly Prayer of Jesus — 17

Discerning the Work God Has Given You — 19

The Kingdom of God Is Advancing By Force — 20

Completing the Work Jesus Has Given Us To Do — 22

J.O. Fraser's Pattern of Prayer Applied to the Lord's Prayer — 24

The Authority of the Christian leader — 27

Kingdom Praying — 35

Daniel Prayer Effort — 36

Yahweh-adonai, The Sovereign LORD — 37

Declaring the Victory of Christ — 39

Serving Notice to the Powers of Darkness — 41

Calling Forth the Harvest — 43

Praying the Prayer of Paul — 44

Kingdom Prayer for Protection — 45

Kingdom Prayer for Sanctification — 47

Kingdom Prayer for Redemption — 48

Notes 53
About the Author 57

Introduction

JOHN THE BAPTIST'S PERSPECTIVE TOWARDS MINISTRY

"A man can receive nothing unless it has been given him from above." John 3:27

This was the response of John the Baptist when his disciples expressed concern that the crowds were leaving them and going after Jesus. John's response was remarkable. Rather than convening a special conference to plan how they could win back the crowds, John expressed this simple truth. God gives success only to the assignments he has given to His servants. And so John's immediate response to his jealous followers was, *"A man can receive nothing unless it has been given him from heaven."*

John then described the picture of a wedding. He made the analogy of Jesus being the bridegroom, the crowds being the bride and himself as the attendant to the bridegroom. John knew his calling. He was not the Christ or the bridegroom. He was the forerunner who prepared the way of the Lord. He was the attendant to the bridegroom. So when he said, "He must increase, I must decrease," John 3:30, John was being true to the assignment God gave him.

Later in the third chapter of John's gospel, John the Baptist described what Jesus was called to do and the reason for His success. "For the One whom God has sent speaks the words of God, for God gives the Spirit without limit. The Father loves the Son and has placed everything in His hands." John 3:34,35

The Father sent Jesus to preach the word of God. The crowds that were now following Jesus were the lost sheep of Israel. The bride that John spoke of was the lost sheep Jesus was addressing. Jesus is able to preach because the Father gave Him the Spirit without measure. The crowds were coming to Jesus because the Father was placing them in His hands. *"A man can receive nothing unless it has been given him from heaven."* John knew that just as the Father placed the crowds in his hands to prepare the way for the Lord, now the Father was placing crowds in Jesus' hands. That is why the crowds were going after Jesus. John had not failed in his mission; rather John had fulfilled it.

The purpose of this booklet is to equip Christian leaders to listen for the calling of the Lord Jesus in their lives and to enter into the work of prayer needed to fulfill that calling. There is an authority and resource available to the Christian leader that can break down the gates of Hades and take ground away from the enemy for the advancement of the Kingdom of the Lord Jesus Christ. The truths of this book have great implication for anyone who has a role of leadership, such as parents, pastors, elders, intercessors, businessmen, Sunday school teachers, small group leaders, evangelists, etc. when they are entrusted by God with the care of others. Any believer who is entrusted with the care of another individual is given authority and resources from the Lord Jesus to minister to that person. It is through the authority of the calling given to the Christian leader and the exercise of that authority through the work of prayer that the Christian leader watches the Lord Jesus build His church and work in the lives of those He has entrusted to him.

A CHILD OF THE FLESH

I was in the pastorate for twenty-five years. If we as pastors were to be honest with one another, we would admit that many of us often compete with each other for greater success. When pastors are introduced to each other, one of the first questions they ask is, "How large is your church?" How many times have pastors grown envious because one has a seemingly more successful ministry (numbers) than the other? The Christian community has lost sight of God's calling. We are competing with one another to have more numbers, rather than seeking to know God's will for our lives, obeying it and then finding joy in accomplishing the work God has given us to do.

Most Christian leaders have had a genuine call from God. They have received promises from the Lord that He is going to use them for His glory. However, they do not patiently wait for the Lord to fulfill His promises to them. They are like Abram who received the promise that he would one day be a great nation, but then took matters into his own hands and Hagar gave birth to Ishmael. Abram ended up with a child born of his own efforts and not of the promise. How many times have Christian leaders received a promise from God that He is going to do something special in their lives, but they can't wait, so they initiate their own plans to try and move things along. Many Christian leaders chase after the latest growth seminar year after year. They take scrupulous notes as they listen to anointed and gifted leaders, and buy the packaged box of program materials. Then they present the materials to their boards and staffs, trying to influence them to change the way they do things in order to produce the same results described at the seminar. The problem is that the gifted and anointed leader is not in the box. As a result, the Christian leader and his organization experience marginal success, often times leaving many dead bodies behind them. When all is said and done, the Christian leader may end up with a child of the flesh and not a child of the promise in his ministry. A year or two passes and he attends another seminar and the cycle is repeated. *"A man can receive nothing unless it has been given him from heaven."* When the Christian leader tries to make things happen in the flesh, he looses sight of the Lord Jesus who fulfills His promises in his life and ministry.

I am not suggesting that the Christian leader does not need mentors or that his attendance at seminars is inappropriate. I praise God for the innumerable spiritual truths I have learned about the Christian life and ministry from the teachings of others through their books and seminars. The Christian leader needs godly men and women who will model obedience and speak into his life, so that he may grow in his love and obedience to Christ and fulfill God's calling in his life. What I am saying is that too often the Christian leader is seeking the success or fruit of another's gifting and anointing, when he should be seeking the Lord Jesus in prayer for His gifting and anointing in his own life.

JESUS THE SOVEREIGN LORD

In his book, Could You Not Tarry for One Hour, Larry Lea instructs his readers to pray through eight compound names[1] of Yahweh. As I have studied the Scriptures, I have discovered and pray through three more compound names of Yahweh. One of those names is Yahweh Adonai, the Sovereign LORD. The sovereignty of God is spoken of often when there is a crisis and it is comforting to know that a good and loving God is in control in times of catastrophe and loss. However I have found that the Sovereign LORD is actually much more intentional, in that He initiates His purposes in the lives of men. Yahweh Adonai, the Sovereign LORD, sets men apart and sends them to accomplish a work. The Sovereign LORD knew Jeremiah before He formed him in the womb. He set Jeremiah apart before he was born. As Jeremiah addressed the Lord he said, "Ah Sovereign Lord, I do not know how to speak; I am only a child." Yet He appointed Jeremiah as a prophet to the nations and kingdoms to uproot and tear down, to destroy and overthrow, to build and to plant. (Jeremiah 1:4-10) The Sovereign LORD brought Ezekiel out by the Spirit of the Lord and set him in the middle of a valley that was full of bones. The Lord asked the prophet if the bones could live. As Ezekiel addressed the Lord he said, "O Sovereign LORD, You alone know." The Sovereign LORD gave the prophet a work to prophecy to the bones that they might be a vast army. (Ez. 37:1-10) In the prophetic passage concerning Jesus' earthly ministry, the Spirit of the Sovereign LORD anointed Him to preach good news to the poor. He sent Jesus,"...to bind up the brokenhearted, to proclaim freedom for the captives and release from darkness for the prisoners, to proclaim the year of the Lord's favor..." Isaiah 61:1-2 In each case the Sovereign LORD is taking the initiative in calling men to accomplish His will.

God the Father was at work as the Sovereign LORD in the life of Jesus. The Father raised Jesus from the dead and seated Him at His right hand. The Father has subjected all things to Jesus. I believe that Jesus, in His oneness with the Father, is the Sovereign LORD in the life of the church today. As the Sovereign LORD, Jesus is very intentional. Jesus is building His church and as the Sovereign LORD, He gives gifts to men to equip the saints to do the work of the ministry. It is Jesus, the Sovereign LORD, who calls men and sends them to do ministry. Jesus gives them the resources to accomplish the ministry He has called them to do. Jesus places people in the hands of those He is calling to minister. Christian ministry is a spiritual work. Why would any Christian leader copy and implement the ministry of another, when Jesus is calling him to a specific work within His kingdom? What makes it so difficult is that leaders are by nature men and women of action. Leaders want to create and administrate the plan of action. Many Christian leaders perceive prayer as passive when in fact it is the work that fulfills the call of the Lord Jesus within the life and ministry of the believer. Jesus invites believers to abide in Him. Jesus promised that if we abide in Him and He abides in us, we would bear much fruit. The pursuit of oneness/abiding with Jesus is realized through prayer. Prayer is the work of the Christian leader where he seeks oneness with Jesus and forcefully asserts the will of Christ in the heavenly realms. This booklet describes the calling of the Christian leader and the work of prayer necessary to complete the work Jesus, the Sovereign LORD, has sent him to do.

Far too often the Christian leader is looking to a program or organization to grow his church rather than the hand of God. As the Christian leader takes time to prayerfully listen, the Lord Jesus reveals the work He is calling him to do. Once the Christian leader senses the work Jesus is calling him to do, he prays a prayer of faith[2] and asks Him for it. Then he steps out in obedience, seeking Jesus' resources to fulfill it. The Christian leader wars in prayer, taking ground away from the enemy. The Christian leader waits for the Lord to place in his hands the fruit of the work He has sent him to do. *"A man can receive nothing unless it has been given him from heaven."*

THE PRIESTLY PRAYER OF JESUS

Jesus gives a glimpse into the oneness He had with the Father in His prayer on the night before He was crucified. When Bible teachers speak on John 17, they often focus on the requests Jesus makes of the Father. However when we understand the setting and the context of Jesus' prayer requests, a partnership between the Father and the Son is found that is remarkable. Sixteen times Jesus used the word "give, gave or given" as He prayed to the Father.

The Father gave Jesus a work to do. Jesus brought the Father glory by completing the work the Father gave Him to do. As I have studied the gospels, I have concluded that there was a fourfold purpose to the work the Father gave to Jesus in His life and death:

1. Proclaim good news to the poor, declare freedom to the captives, recovery of sight to the blind and release the oppressed (Luke 4:18),
2. Train the twelve disciples (Matt. 4:19),
3. Give His life a ransom for many (Matt. 20:28), and
4. Destroy the works of the devil (1John 3:8).

The Father sent Jesus and gave Him this fourfold work. Jesus brought glory to the Father by completing the work. Jesus is now praying and asks the Father to glorify Himself. (John 17:4,5) The Father also gave Jesus five resources in order to accomplish that work. Four of these resources are identified in Jesus' prayer in John 17. With each resource given from the Father, Jesus ministered to those the Father gave Him. Jesus knows that in a little while He will leave His disciples and so He is praying for them as He prepares to leave.

1. *The Father gave Jesus His authority (v 2).* Jesus gave eternal life to all those the Father had given to Him (v 2). Jesus sent them into the world (v 18). He is now praying for those who will believe through His disciples and asks that they might be one (v 21).

2. *The Father gave Jesus His words (v 8).* Jesus revealed the Father to those the Father gave to Him (v 6). Jesus gave them the words the Father gave to Him (v 8). Jesus now prays for them and asks the Father that His disciples will be where He is (v 24). Jesus promised that He would make Himself known to His disciples and continue to make Himself known (v. 26).

3. *The Father gave Jesus His name (v 11,12).* Jesus protected those who the Father gave Him and kept them safe by the power of the name the Father gave Him (v 12). Jesus also sanctified Himself that they might be sanctified (v 19). Jesus is now praying and asks the Father to protect them by the power of that name so that they might be one (v 11). Jesus again prays and asks the Father to protect them from the evil one (v 15). Finally, Jesus prays and asks the Father to sanctify them in the truth (v 17).

4. *The Father gave Jesus His glory (v 22,24).* Jesus gave His glory to those the Father gave Him that they might be one (v 22). Jesus now prays and asks the Father that they would be where He is and they would see His glory (v 24).

The fifth resource the Father gave Jesus is found in John the Baptist's words concerning Jesus in John 3:34,35. It is the ministry of the Holy Spirit:

5. *The Father gave Jesus the Spirit without limit.* Jesus spoke the word of God. "For the one whom God has sent speaks the words of God, for God gives the Spirit without limit. The Father loves the Son and has placed everything in His hands." John 3:34,35

Jesus is building His church. He gives gifts to men. As the Sovereign LORD, Jesus is sending His followers to minister in the same way the Father sent Him. Jesus said, "As You sent Me into the world, I have sent them into the world." John 17:18. Just as the Father gave Jesus a work to do, Jesus is giving believers a work to do. Once a believer has listened for and discerned the work that Jesus is giving to him, it is a matter of obedience to step out and fulfill the work Jesus has sent him to do. In the same way, the Father gave Jesus resources to accomplish the work He gave Jesus to do, Jesus gives the believer His authority, His words, His name, His glory and His Spirit in order to accomplish the work Jesus has given to him. It is only through these resources that a Christian leader will have the wisdom and power to fulfill the Lord's will in his life. Just as the Father placed people into the hands of Jesus, Jesus is entrusting people to the Christian leader's care. It is as the Christian leader has an open hand and allows the Lord to place everything He wishes in his hand that the Christian leader receives the promise of Jesus' calling in his life and ministry. *"A man can receive nothing unless it has been given him from heaven."* These words were true in the lives of John the Baptist and Jesus, and they are true in the life of the Christian leader today.

DISCERNING THE WORK GOD HAS GIVEN YOU
AND THE PEOPLE HE IS PLACING IN YOUR HANDS

So what is the work Jesus, the Sovereign LORD, has give to you? I find that different people respond to different questions as they seek to discern God's calling in their lives. I may ask one person, "What is God's calling in your life?" He will immediately respond with a brief and concise answer. However, many see God's calling as something their pastor or a missionary has, not themselves. Through the years I have assisted many followers of Christ to discern the work and people the Lord Jesus has given them to do through the following six questions:

1. What breaths life into your soul?
2. What passion has the Lord Jesus placed on your heart?
3. What promises has the Jesus given to you?
4. Who are the people the Lord has placed in your hands?
5. What tasks or things is the Sovereign Lord entrusting to you?
6. What are the gifts and anointings mature believers see in your life and ministry that bear fruit for the Kingdom of God?

I suggest they prayerfully and thoughtfully answer each question that they connect with. Not every question will be for them. I then suggest they write out in one or two sentences a statement that defines the work and people Jesus, the Sovereign LORD, is placing in their hands. I realize that for many, they could write a one to three page explanation of God's calling in their lives. Their calling may be multifaceted. I in no way want to diminish the importance or the impact of God's calling in their lives. I think there is benefit in creating a simple and concise statement. Especially for the purpose of warfare prayer.

THE KINGDOM OF GOD IS ADVANCING BY FORCE

Jesus is building His church and the gates of Hades will not prevail against it. When Jesus speaks of building His church, He speaks of spiritual warfare in the same breath. It is interesting to note that both Jesus and John the Baptist engaged in spiritual warfare as they fulfilled their calling. While John was in prison he sent his disciples to Jesus to inquire if He was the Messiah. Jesus told them to return to John and tell him what they saw and heard. After John's disciples left, Jesus spoke to the crowds concerning John. In the course of His comments, Jesus made a statement about spiritual warfare; "From the days of John the Baptist until now, the kingdom of heaven has been forcefully advancing, and forceful men lay hold of it." Matt. 11:12 John and Jesus advanced the kingdom of heaven by force and as forceful men they laid hold of it. The devil is the prince of this world. As John the Baptist came to prepare the way of the Lord, he was taking ground away from the devil, the prince of this world. In the same way, as Jesus came to preach good news to the poor, proclaim freedom for the prisoners, and recovery of sight for the blind, to release the oppressed and proclaim the year of the Lord's favor He was taking ground away from the prince of this world.

Although we do not see any confrontations of John the Baptist with the devil in prayer, there are five different passages in Scripture that would indicate a confrontation did take place between Jesus and the devil in prayer. In each of these confrontations, Jesus is either taking ground away from the prince of this world or He is protecting ground that has been gained.

1. In Luke 4:1-13, the devil challenged Jesus' role as the Son of God in the wilderness. The Son threatens the devil, because the Father promised to give Him the nations as an inheritance and the ends of the earth as His possession (Ps. 2:6-9). As Jesus fasted for forty days, He found the spiritual power to be a forceful man and resisted the devil in prayer, using the word of God to confront each temptation. Jesus was doing the work of prayer needed to take ground away from the prince of this world in his public ministry.

2. In Matt 12:24-29, the Pharisees accused Jesus of casting out demons by Beelzebub, the prince of demons. Jesus responded with the spiritual principle of binding the strong man. Why would Jesus even state such a principle, unless it was true of Himself? I believe that Jesus, as a forceful man, bound the strong man in the temptation in the wilderness as He fasted. That is why He was able to cast out demons and take ground away from the strong man in His ministry.

3. In Luke 10:17-19, the seventy-two returned from the mission Jesus sent them on. They were rejoicing because even the demons submitted to them in the name of Jesus. Jesus responded by telling them that He saw Satan fall like lightning from heaven. I want to suggest that Jesus, as a forceful man, warred in prayer for the seventy-two. As they ministered, they were taking ground away from Satan and he fell out of heaven.

4. In Luke 22:31,32, Satan wanted to sift Simon Peter as wheat. Jesus, as a forceful man, prayed for Simon. Although Simon denied Jesus on the night He was betrayed, Simon's faith did not fail, unlike Judas who betrayed Jesus hanged himself. Jesus would not let Satan take the ground back from Him.

5. In John 17:11,12, Jesus, as a forceful man, prays for those the Father gave Him and protects them by the power of the name

the Father gave Him. Jesus protected the ground (those the Father gave to Him) from the evil one through prayer.

Jesus advanced the Kingdom of God by force. When He spoke of building His church, He said the gates of Hades would not prevail against it. Jesus is speaking of a spiritual warfare that will take place as He builds His church in the future.

When the Christian leader senses that the Lord Jesus is giving him a work to do and he responds in obedience to Jesus' call, he can expect to be attacked by the evil one. The devil is threatened by the one who is called and steps out in obedience to complete the work the Lord Jesus has given him to do. As the Christian leader obeys God's call, there is a work of prayer to be done. If the Christian leader is going to be Christ-like in obeying God's call, he will be a forceful man and advance the Kingdom of God by force through prayer.

COMPLETING THE WORK JESUS HAS GIVEN US TO DO

One of my historical mentors, J.O. Fraser, was a missionary to China one hundred years ago. He preached the gospel to the Lisu tribes people of the mountains of southwest China that border Myanmar (Burma). After many years of ministry and prayer, he experienced a people movement where entire villages responded to the claims of Christ. In his biography, <u>Behind The Ranges</u>, J.O. Fraser writes a letter[1] to his prayer partners describing the process of accomplishing the work God gave him through prayer.

In his letter, JO Fraser makes a correlation between the Christian leader in the spiritual harvest field of China and the migrant farmer in harvest fields of the plains of Canada. He said that once a believer discerns the ground (the work and people) God is giving him he needs to pray a deliberate prayer of faith. This definite[2] prayer of faith is like the migrant farmer staking a claim with the local government officials for the land assigned to him. So for JO Fraser asked God to give him the ground (dozens of Lisu tribes families) that He has assigned to Him.

JO Fraser continues with this analogy of the Christian leader in the spiritual harvest field and the migrant farm worker in the plains of Canada and suggests that once the claim is made the migrant farm worker had to get to work[3]. Although the Canadian government might give incentives for the migrant worker to travel to the plains and give them land. The migrant worker was now responsible for the work. The government was not going to work the land for him. He had to till the soil, plant the seed and harvest the crop. And so it is for the Christian leader. He is called to make disciples and throughout the discipleship process there is a work of prayer to be done. JO Fraser suggests that there is a rest as well as a wrestling in the work. On the one hand, the Christian leader knows that Jesus, the Sovereign Lord, has given him the land (work and people) in this spiritual harvest field. *A man can have nothing unless it is given to him from heaven.* On the other hand there is a wrestling when praying through to victory for the discipleship process of men and women becoming followers of Christ and workers in the harvest field.

Once there has been a definite prayer of faith concerning the work Jesus, the Sovereign Lord, has given us to do and those He is placing in our hands, there is no need to ask for the ground over and over again. Yet there is a wrestling in prayer with the powers of darkness. J. O. Fraser suggested that there is a work of prayer that would take the following form[4]:

1. A firm standing on God-given ground, and a constant assertion of faith and claiming of victory. He found it helpful to repeat passages of Scripture applicable to the subject. He felt that faith needed to be continually strengthened and fed from its proper source, the Word of God.

2. A definite fighting and resisting against Satan's host in the name of Christ. As direct weapons against Satan, Fraser would read in prayer such passages as I John 3:8, "The reason the Son of God appeared was to destroy the devil's work." and

Revelation 12:11, "They overcame him by the blood of the Lamb."

3. Praying through every aspect of the matter in detail. In the case of his Lisu work, Fraser continually prayed to God for a fresh knowledge of His will. He desired more wisdom in dealing with the people, knowledge of how to pray, help in studying the language, etc.

In praying this way, J.O. Fraser watched the Lord Jesus bring about a people movement among the Lisu tribesmen. He tells one story where he was sharing the gospel in a village called Middle Village[5]. The heads of thirteen families met to discuss whether or not they should turn Christian. Their decision was against it because of two men. That afternoon he went to a neighboring village where he found an empty room. The Lord met with him and encouraged his heart. The next day, Fraser gave himself to prayer in that empty room. He fought against principalities and powers for Middle Village. The next day he returned to Middle Village and shared the gospel once again. This time the leaders were much more responsive. Eleven of the thirteen families responded in faith in Christ. It was the work of prayer, confronting the powers of darkness in that empty room that made the difference in the lives of eleven families in Middle Village.

J. O. FRASER'S PATTERN OF PRAYER APPLIED TO THE LORD'S PRAYER

The Lord's Prayer is a helpful prayer pattern for a Christian leader as he enters into the warfare prayer needed to fulfill the work that Jesus, the Sovereign Lord, has sent him to do. The first thing the Christian leader must do is come to a place of abiding where he appropriates the present ministry of Jesus by asking Jesus to set Himself apart as Yahweh[1]. There are eleven different compound names of Yahweh[2] that a believer can pray through to appropriate the present ministry of Jesus in his life and ministry. In the Kingdom

Praying section of this book you will find one Yahweh[3] prayer that many have found helpful in coming to a place of abiding in order that the Christian leader may be in the place of intercession, seated with Christ in the heavenly realms, that is needed to do the work of prayer.

Specifically, the Christian leader asks the Lord Jesus to set Himself apart as Yahweh Adonai, the Sovereign Lord. Jesus is building His church. Jesus gives gifts to men. He sends His followers as the Father sent Him to accomplish the work He has called them to do. In faith, the Christian leader affirms:

1. The work the Sovereign Lord Jesus has given him to do,
2. The resources Jesus is giving him to accomplish the work, and
3. Those people and/or things Jesus is placing in his hands.

The Christian leader should often quote the Scripture verses, pray through the word pictures or sing the songs the Lord has given him as promises of His sovereign call in his life. The Christian leader finds a twofold benefit in this affirmation of asking the Lord Jesus to set Himself apart as Yahweh Adonai, the Sovereign Lord:

1. He is appropriating the work of Jesus as the builder of His church in his life and ministry. *"A man can receive nothing unless it has been given him from heaven."*
2. His faith is encouraged through affirming the promises[4] the Lord has given him in his life and calling.

In all of this the Christian leader is standing firm on his God-given ground, making a persistent assertion of faith and claiming the victory. In that place of abiding the Christian leader is:

1. One with Jesus being seated with Christ as a member of His body in the heavenly realms,
2. Loving Jesus and keeping His commands, and
3. Connected to the Head of the church and listening for His mind.

In the place of abiding/oneness with Jesus, the Christian leader is in a place of authority and intercession at the right hand of the Father. As one who has been given a work to do and is sent by the Sovereign Lord Jesus, the Christian leader takes hold of the authority that has been given to him. He prays Kingdom prayers, entering into spiritual warfare to take ground away from the enemy and advance the Kingdom of God. In doing this:

1. Jesus gives the Christian leader His authority that he might minister to those Jesus has given to him. This means the Christian leader:

    a. Declares the victory of Christ in His life, death, resurrection and ascension[5],

    b. Serves notice[6] to demonic strongholds, declaring what Jesus is going to do, and

    c. Calls forth a harvest[7] of laborers and persons of peace to join him in the harvest and those lost households the Lord Jesus is placing in his hands.

2. Jesus gives the Christian leader His words, so that he might give revelation to those Jesus has entrusted to him. The Christian leader prays for the ministry of the Holy Spirit to reveal spiritual realities, using the prayers of Paul for himself and those Jesus has given to him for:

    a. Encounters with God and the spiritual realities that describe their position in Christ, (Ephesians 1:17-19)

    b. Strength in the inner person to know the presence of Jesus and the love of God, (Ephesians 3:16-19) and

    c. Guidance and direction to know what to do and how to do it as he completes the work the Lord Jesus has given him to do. (Colossians 1:9-12)

3. Jesus gives the Christian leader His name that he might protect those Jesus has entrusted to him. The Christian leader prays that Jesus will:

a. As the Lord of hosts, send His angels to protect those Jesus has entrusted to him, so that they would be one,

   b. As the author and perfecter of faith, sanctify those Jesus has given to him, as they experience the hardships of life and study His word.

4. Jesus gives the Christian leader His glory that he might give it to those Jesus has given to him that they might be one. The Christian leader prays that his followers will be one with the Father and Son that they might be perfected in unity.

THE AUTHORITY OF THE CHRISTIAN LEADER

There has been much confusion and abuse concerning the exercise of authority by Christian leaders within the Christian community. The very moment the Christian leader asserts his authority over an individual to control his behavior, he has lost sight of the model of Jesus as He exercised authority. At that moment, the Christian leader needs to step back and be still. *"A man can receive nothing unless it has been given him from heaven."* It is the Spirit's job to move men and women to action. The Christian leader can cast vision but the moment he begins to manipulate or control someone he has lost sight of true Biblical authority. Spiritual authority is given in order to protect from the devil those God has given to the Christian leader. Spiritual authority is an opportunity to serve those under the Christian leader's care; guiding, empowering and releasing them to be everything God has called and gifted them to be.

What does the Scripture have to say about spiritual authority? First of all, God is the one who gives spiritual authority to the Christian leader. (John 17:2; Mark 6:7; Luke 10:17-19) As a result, the Christian leader who has been given authority seeks to please the One who has given that authority to him. (John 5:30) Second, although the Christian leader is seated with Christ in the heavenly realms and has been given a place of authority, the scope of his spiritual authority is limited to the work the Lord Jesus has called him to do and the individuals the Lord is placing in his hands. (John 17:1-2) Third, the primary purpose of spiritual authority is for spiritual warfare against the powers of darkness that seek to hinder the advancement of the Kingdom of God and harm those the Lord has entrusted to the Christian leader. (Luke 22:31,32) Finally, the Christian leader is not to lord his authority over those Jesus has entrusted to him. Rather, his position of authority is an opportunity to serve those the Lord has placed in his hands. (Matt. 20:20-28; Mark 10:35-45; John 13:1-5)

As Jesus speaks of His own authority, He says that the Father gave Him authority over all men in order that He might give eternal life to all those the Father gave Him. Although Jesus had authority over all men, He chose to limit the exercise of that authority to those the Father was entrusting to Him. (John 17:2) In the Gospels we see that Jesus had authority to:

- drive out evil spirits, (Mark 1:27; Luke 4:36)
- forgive sins, (Matt. 9:6; Mark 2:10; Luke 5:24)
- judge, (John 5:26-30)
- lay down his life and to take it up again, (John 10:14-18) and
- give eternal life. (John 17:1-3)

Jesus also gave authority to the twelve and the seventy-two when He appointed them and sent them out to minister. As the Father gave Jesus authority when He sent Jesus, so Jesus gave His disciples authority to:

- drive out evil spirits, (Matt. 10:1; Mark 3:15; Luke 9:1)
- heal every disease and sickness, (Matt. 10:1; Luke 9:1) and
- overcome all the power of the enemy. (Mark 6:7; Luke 10:17-19)

In the epistles, we see that the resurrected and ascended Christ had been exalted to a position of authority in heaven far above all angelic beings, both righteous and fallen. (Eph. 1:19-23) At the very name of Jesus, every knee will bow and every tongue will confess that He is Lord. (Phil. 2:9-11) The believer, as a member of the body of Christ, is seated with Jesus. All things have been placed under the feet of Jesus and because the believer is seated with Christ, all things have been placed under the believer's feet as well. (Eph. 1:22,23) Jesus said that all authority in heaven and earth had been given to Him. As a result, Jesus commissioned the twelve to make disciples. (Matt. 28:18-20)

As the Sovereign Lord, Jesus is building His church and He gives gifts to men. Jesus chooses, calls and sends the Christian leader to do ministry. He gives the Christian leader authority to accomplish that ministry. The very position of the believer seated with Christ in the heavenly realms is a place of authority. The believer has been made alive, raised and seated with Christ in the heavenly realms and all things are placed under his feet as a member of Christ's body. Although a believer has a position of authority seated with Christ in the heavenly realms, the scope of his authority is the work Jesus has given him to do and those individuals Jesus has placed in his hands. Let me warn all who will enter into spiritual warfare that it is a dangerous thing to assert spiritual authority over anything other than the sphere of work the Lord Jesus has given to the Christian leader. The Christian leader has spiritual authority over all those who God has entrusted to his care, whether that leader be a parent, grandparent, home group leader, Sunday school class leader or teacher, children's teacher, intercessor, businessman, youth intern, ministerial staff or pastor.

If the Lord Jesus has given the Christian leader responsibility for someone, then he will also give him spiritual authority over the demonic powers that would seek to intrude into his life and have legal ground over him. Jesus gives authority to the Christian leader, and as a result, the Christian leader seeks to please Jesus, the Head of the body. The Christian leader follows the Spirit of Truth's guidance as he exerts his authority in prayer, warring against the powers of darkness that seek to harm those Jesus has entrusted to him. The Christian leader asserts authority with a spoken word in prayer while seated with Jesus in the heavenly realms in his prayer closet and/or in times of ministry. Through exerting authority by declaring the victory of Christ, serving notice to the powers of darkness, and declaring what Jesus is going to do over a period of time, the Christian leader gains a position of authority[1] over the powers of darkness. After all, Jesus fasted for forty days to gain a position of authority of the devil. The gates of Hades will no longer prevail. A door of ministry is opened. The Christian leader takes ground away from the enemy and the Kingdom of God is advanced by force. As the Christian leader maintains his place of abiding/oneness with Jesus, the head of the body, the anointing of the Spirit rests upon him to fulfill God's calling and to bear fruit for the glory of God throughout his ministry.

There are two extremes when it comes to exerting spiritual authority. One extreme for the Christian leader is not to exert any spiritual authority on behalf of those Jesus has entrusted to him. As a result, their followers are vulnerable to the attacks of the enemy. Only in heaven will we learn how many followers of Christ fell short of the grace of God through a bitter spirit and the resulting divisiveness, immorality, and/or godlessness due to the prayerlessness of those in spiritual authority over them. At the very least, many are suffering from spiritual anemia because those in spiritual authority over them never asserted their spiritual authority and prayed for the protection of those Jesus entrusted to them.

The other extreme is to assert authority over the powers of darkness outside the sphere of the work Jesus has given the Christian leader to do. I have watched many pastors and Christian leaders assert their authority as believers seated with Christ in the heavenly realms, binding the strongholds and/or declaring truth of what Jesus is going to do over their city when they were not given that assignment from the Lord. Their lives, families and ministries came under great attack in the months and years that followed. My sense is that the calamity they experienced was the result of stepping outside of God's calling in their lives. You may question, "Wow, if that is so, than why even enter into this kind of spiritual warfare?" The

Christian leader enters into spiritual warfare because it is a reality in the Christian life and Kingdom ministry. If the Christian leader is going to be one with Jesus as He builds His church and fulfills the work that Jesus has given him to do, he will enter into spiritual warfare in the sphere of his calling. When praying with others in a prayer gathering for an area that is outside the sphere of his calling, I would suggest that the Christian leader limit his prayers to supplication for the ministry of angels and the Holy Spirit and the appropriation of the present ministry of Jesus by praying through the names of Yahweh.

The Christian leader's authority is an opportunity to serve those Jesus has entrusted to him and is never to be lorded over them. When a Christian leader asserts that he has been given spiritual authority over someone, he needs to ask four questions:

1. Have I assumed spiritual responsibility for the soul of this person?
2. Do I pray for the ministry of the Holy Spirit to give him encounters with Jesus and guidance into Jesus' will for his life?
3. Do I keep watch over him in prayer and war against the schemes and works of the evil one to hold him in bondage?
4. Do I serve this person, empowering and releasing him to be everything God has called him and gifted him to be?

"A man can receive nothing unless it has been given him from heaven."

Christian ministry is a grace work. It is the Sovereign Lord who calls men and women to ministry. It is the Sovereign Lord who gives the resources to fulfill that ministry. And it is the Sovereign Lord who places the fruit of that ministry (people) in our hands. When examining the ministry of Jesus, a oneness is revealed between the Father and the Son. A spiritual warfare is also revealed as Jesus, a forceful man in prayer, advances the Kingdom of God by force. Whether the Christian leader is a parent, pastor, intercessor, businessman or worker within a church, the role of leadership is only fulfilled by the grace of God. It is the Sovereign Lord who calls the Christian leader. It is the work of Christ on the cross that has given him a place of intercession. It is the power of the Spirit that enables him to confront the powers of darkness. Has the ministry the Lord Jesus has called you to become a child of the flesh or a child of the promise? If it has become a child of the flesh. It is time to be still and listen for the call of the Sovereign Lord Jesus. It is time to take hold of the resources Jesus has given to accomplish His calling in your life. It is time to stop striving and enter into His rest. It is time to stop manipulating those the Lord has entrusted to you, and to serve them and let Jesus fulfill His promises in your life and ministry. *"A man can receive nothing unless it has been given him from heaven."* Jesus is building His church. The gates of Hades cannot prevail against it. He is calling you and giving you authority to be a part of His work.

God met with Abram and called him to leave his family and go to the land that He would show him. Abram obeyed the Lord and arrived in the land of Canaan at age 75. God and Abram met with one another repeatedly for the next 11 years. Abram was called God's friend. (James 2:23) He was a man who sought after the Lord as he built altars in different locations and called on the name of the Lord. (Gen. 12:7,8; 13:4, 18) Through those years, Abram watched the Lord rescue him from poor choices and honor his good choices. However, when Sarai could not conceive a child and offered her handmaid to Abram, he took matters into his own hands and a child of the flesh was born when Abram was 86 years old. For the next thirteen years, Abram did not hear a word from God. Then at age 99 Abram had an encounter with the Lord. The Lord said to him, *"I am God Almighty; walk before me and be blameless. I will confirm my covenant between me and you and will greatly increase your numbers."* Gen 17:1 As God meets with Abram after thirteen years of silence, the first thing He says is, *"I am God Almighty* (El Shaddai).*"* The Lord is saying to Abram, "I can do this, I am the All-Sufficient One." Then El Shaddai affirms His promise to Abram that Sarai will conceive and give birth to a son. The Lord was restoring His servant and affirming His covenant with him. Abram's response was notable. Abram fell face down before the Lord. He then responded immediately in obedience to the Lord's direction. Within the year, Sarai is with child and the child of the promise is born to Abraham and Sarah. You may find yourself presently in a place of frustration. You once heard God's call, but you took matters into your own hands and as a result you have given birth to a child of the flesh. However, you long for a child of the promise. Let this moment be God's encounter with you. The Lord is God Almighty, El Shaddai! He will fulfill His calling in your life. Let Him restore you. Respond to Him. Fall facedown before Him and listen for His voice. Step out in obedience to His call and enter into the work of prayer that will accomplish His work in your life and ministry. *"A man can receive nothing unless has been given him from heaven."*

Kingdom Praying

DANIEL PRAYER EFFORT

(A Daniel Prayer Effort is a tool to discern the work the Lord Jesus has given you to do and the people He is placing in your hands.)

What is a Daniel Prayer Effort?

A Daniel Prayer Effort[1] is a spiritual discipline of prayer where a believer seeks God's direction over a twenty-one day period. It is modeled after Daniel of the Old Testament. Daniel received a vision from the Lord. When he could not interpret the vision, Daniel humbled himself before the Lord and sought His guidance through fasting. Daniel entered into a moderate fast for twenty-one days until he received a visitation from an angel. The angel was sent from God and gave him the interpretation of the vision. A Daniel Prayer Effort is:

1. A persistent seeking of the presence of God. (Jer. 29:12-14)
2. A persistent listening to the Holy Spirit for: (Jn 16:13-15)
    a. 1. Guidance into all truth,
    b. 2. Revelation of what is yet to come, and
    c. 3. Knowledge of what belongs to Jesus.

How does a Daniel Prayer Effort work?

When a believer is faced with a major decision or is in need of insight from God into a very difficult situation, he is ready for a Daniel Prayer Effort.

The believer draws near to God in prayer daily for twenty-one days through journaling. While journaling the believer expresses his:

1. Feelings about the situation he is facing,
2. Desire to meet with the Lord and know His presence,
3. Desire to lay down his plans and agenda, and
4. Questions concerning the situation confronting him.

After he journals these thoughts, he listens for the Holy Spirit's direction. He sets his pen down and waits for the Spirit's leading. John Regier, the Director of Biblical Concepts in Counseling in Colorado Springs, suggests that a believer may hear God through:

1. A passage of Scripture,
2. A song,
3. A word picture,
4. Insightful thoughts, and/or
5. New questions.

Over the course of the twenty-one day period, the questions may change. New insight might be given into what Jesus is doing. The Lord may deal with several spiritual formation issues within the life of the one praying. It is essential to make sure all insight received is aligned with Scripture. In addition, confirmation by one's spouse, family members, and mature mentors is important.

"A man can receive nothing unless it has been given him from heaven."

Yahweh-adonai, (ad e' ni) The Sovereign LORD[1]

When Ezekiel, the prophet, was led into a valley of dry bones, God commands the prophet to prophesy to the dry bones. Ezekiel declared the name of God and says, *"This is what* Yahweh-adonai, the Sovereign LORD *says: 'Come from the four winds, O breath, and breathe into these slain, that they may live.'"* The following is a prayer appropriating the name of Yahweh-adonai, the Sovereign LORD and the present ministry of Jesus as the builder of His church in the life of a Christian leader.

Who am I? A man can have nothing unless it is given to him from above. Lord Jesus, You are Yahweh-adonai, the Sovereign LORD. You are building Your church and just as the Father sent You, so You are sending me.

Lord Jesus, the Spirit of the Sovereign Lord was upon You. In Your earthly ministry, the Spirit anointed You to preach good news to the poor, to proclaim freedom to the prisoners, to bind up the broken hearted, to give recovery of sight to the blind, and to release from darkness the oppressed.

The Father gave you a work to preach the word of God to the lost sheep of Israel, to train the twelve, to give Your life as a ransom for many and to destroy the works of the devil. You brought glory to the Father by completing the work He gave You. The Father gave You the resources to complete the work. The Father gave you authority that You might give eternal life to all those He had given to You. The Father gave you His words that You might give His words to those He entrusted You. You protected those the Father gave You by the power of the name He gave you that they might be one. You gave them the glory that the Father gave You that they might be one. The Father gave You the Spirit without limit. Because He loved You, the Father placed all things in Your hands. All that You had was the Father's and all that the Father had was Yours. None of Your followers had been lost except the one doomed to destruction, so that Scripture would be fulfilled.

You were raised from the dead and when You ascended to heaven, You gave gifts to men. Now You are building Your church. As the Father sent You, You sent Your disciples.

Who am I that I should serve You, the living God? Lord Jesus, set Yourself apart as Yahweh Adonai, the Sovereign Lord. You are building Your church. As the Father sent You, You are sending me. I affirm that You have given me this work of _____ to do. *(Affirm Jesus' calling in your life, quoting the scriptures, praying through the themes of the word pictures or singing the songs he has given to you.)*

I ask in Your name, Lord Jesus that You anoint me with Your Spirit today just as the Father anointed You. Just as the Father loved You and placed all things in Your hands, I affirm that You love me and are giving to me Your authority that I may minister to those You are entrusting to me. I affirm that You are giving me Your words that I may give them to those You are giving to me. You are giving me Your name that I may protect those in prayer that You are entrusting to me. I affirm that You are giving me Your glory that I may give it to them. Lord Jesus, all that I have is Yours and all that You have is mine. I affirm that You are giving _____ to me. *(Affirm the who and what of the people the Lord Jesus is entrusting to you.)*

Build Your church, Lord Jesus! Set Yourself apart as Yahweh-adonai, the Sovereign LORD, in my life. In Your name, I pray! Amen.

DECLARING THE VICTORY OF CHRIST
IN HIS LIFE, DEATH, RESURRECTION AND ASCENSION

(Using the declaration of the victory of Christ[1] in His life, death, resurrection and ascension, assert the authority of the Lord Jesus over the work the Sovereign LORD has given you to do and the people He is placing in your hands.)

Let Your Kingdom come, Father God! Let Your will be done on earth as it is in heaven! In the authority of the name of Jesus, by the redemptive power of Your blood, and in the power of the Holy Spirit, I declare the victory of Your Son's life, death, resurrection and ascension over _____ !

I declare the victory of Jesus' life! Your Son never yielded to the devil. The prince of this world never had a hold on Him, but He always loved You and did exactly what You, Father, commanded. Your Son overcame the world and now the prince of this world stands condemned. Now we have overcome the world through our faith in Your Son. Let Your Kingdom come! Let Your will be done in _____ , as it is in heaven!

I declare the victory of Jesus' death! Your Son is the seed of the woman who came to crush the head of the serpent. He bruised Your Son's heel, but Jesus crushed his head. Jesus shared in the likeness of our flesh that He might destroy him who has the power of death, that is the devil. He disarmed every power and authority in the heavenly realms. Jesus made a public display of them and triumphed over them by His cross. Now we are overcomers by the blood of the Lamb. I declare the victory of Your Son's death over __ _____ ! Let Your Kingdom come! Let Your will be done on earth as it is in heaven!

I declare the victory of Your Son's resurrection, Father God! You exerted the strength of Your might when You raised Jesus from the dead! You declared with power that Jesus is the Son of God by the resurrection of the dead. As the Son, Jesus came for the purpose to destroy the works of the devil. As the Son, Jesus, is building His church and the gates of Hades will not prevail against it. I declare the victory of Your Son's resurrection! Let Your Kingdom come! Let Your will be done in _____ , as it is in heaven!

I declare the victory of Your Son's ascension! I declare that You exerted the strength of Your might when You seated Jesus at Your right hand far above all rulers, powers, authorities and dominions and every name that can be named in this age and the age to come. You placed all things under Jesus' feet. I declare that You gave Jesus a name that is above every name. At His name, "Jesus," every knee shall bow and every tongue shall confess that Your Son, Jesus, is Lord! I declare that _____ has been made alive, raised and seated with Jesus in the heavenly realms. As members of the Body of Christ, they are seated with Your Son and You have placed every agent of the enemy under their feet! I declare the victory of the Your Son's ascension, Holy Father! Let Your Kingdom come! Let Your will be done!

In the authority of the name of Jesus, by the redemptive power of His blood and in the power of the Holy Spirit, I declare the victory of the Lord Jesus Christ in His life, death, resurrection and ascension in the heavenly realms! Your lord never had a hold on my Lord, but my Lord always loved the Father and did exactly what He commanded! My Lord overcame the world and now your lord, the prince of this world stands condemned!

I declare that my Lord, the Lord Jesus Christ, destroyed your master at the cross! Your lord bruised the heel of my Lord, but my Lord crushed the head of your lord! My Lord disarmed you! He made a public display of you and triumphed over you by His cross!

I declare that my Lord was declared with power to be the Son of God by the resurrection of the dead and as the Son, He came to destroy every work of the devil set up against _____ ! My Lord is building His church and the gates of Hades cannot prevail against it!

My Lord has been seated at the right hand of the Father far above you, your master, and all rulers, powers, authorities and dominions in the heavenly realms! The Father has placed all things under Jesus' feet. You are but a footstool for the feet of Jesus! At the name of my Lord, "Jesus," you must bow your knee and confess that Jesus is Lord! Bow your knee at the name of Jesus! Holy Father, let Your Kingdom come! Let Your will be done in _____ as it is in heaven! In Jesus' name I pray! Amen!

(If you are uncomfortable with addressing demonic powers, you may want to pray just the first five paragraphs of this warfare prayer.)

SERVING NOTICE TO THE POWERS OF DARKNESS

(Using the Serving Notice To The Powers Of Darkness prayer, declare what the Lord Jesus is going to do and serve notice[1] to the powers of darkness.)

Holy Father, let Your Kingdom come! Let Your will be done on earth as it is in Heaven! In the authority of the name of Jesus, by the redemptive power of His blood and in the power of the Holy Spirit, I declare that Jesus is building His church and your gates cannot stand against it!

In that realm where I am seated with Jesus and as one called of the Lord, I declare that Jesus is _____! *(Declare the details of the work Jesus has given to you, quoting the Scriptures and claiming the promises the Lord Jesus has given to you.)*

I serve you notice! My Lord, the Lord Jesus Christ, has destroyed the works of the devil and so, by the blood of the Lamb, I cancel every scheme and work of the evil one set up against _____! You must bow your knee at the name of Jesus! Stop your wicked work and bow your knee, in Jesus name! Jesus is building His church and your gates cannot prevail against it! Let Your Kingdom come! Let Your will be done on earth as it is in Heaven, Holy Father!

(The following is an example of serving notice to the powers of darkness, declaring the work Jesus has given to the Prayer Director of MentorLink)

Holy Father, let Your Kingdom come! Let Your will be done on earth as it is in Heaven! In the authority of the name of Jesus, by the redemptive power of His blood and in the power of the Holy Spirit, I declare that Jesus is building His church and your gates cannot stand against it!

In that realm where I am seated with Jesus and as one called of the Lord:

- I declare that Jesus is giving life to dry bones and He is raising up a vast army of intercessors to pray for the Kingdom.

- I declare that the Lord Jesus has called me to mobilize, equip and resource intercessors to pray for the Kingdom of God.

- I declare that Jesus is setting the captives free, mending the broken hearted and releasing the oppressed that they might serve the living God and fulfill the work that Jesus has given them to do!

I serve you notice! My Lord, the Lord Jesus Christ has destroyed the works of the devil, your lord, and so, by the blood of the Lamb, I cancel every scheme and work of the evil one set up against the pastors, business owners, ministry leaders to keep them from praying for their ministry and fulfilling the work Jesus has given them to do! You must bow at the name of Jesus! Stop your wicked work and bow your knee, in Jesus name! Jesus is building His church and your gates cannot prevail against it! Let Your Kingdom come! Let Your will be done on earth as it is in Heaven, Holy Father!

CALLING FORTH THE HARVEST

(Using the Calling Forth The Harvest[1] prayer, call forth a harvest of those laborers and persons of peace the Lord Jesus is placing in your hands.)

Father God, let Your Kingdom come! Let Your will be done on earth as it is in Heaven! In the authority of the name of the Lord Jesus, by the redemptive power of His blood and in the power or the Holy Spirit I declare that Jesus is building His church and your gates cannot prevail against it!

Holy Father, in Jesus' name, I ask You to bring laborers to accomplish this Kingdom work You have called me to. Father, bring persons of peace who will share the good news of the Kingdom to their community, in Jesus' name! Bring _____ *(Name the specific laborers you need to fulfill the work Jesus has given you.)* from the east, the west, the north and the south. Gather everyone who is called by Your name, those You created for Your glory, those You formed and made, in Jesus' name!

In the name of Jesus, I command every scheme and every work of the enemy who holds them back to let them go! You are but a footstool for the feet of Jesus. Jesus is building His church and you must let them go, in Jesus' name!

Let Your Kingdom come! Let Your will be done! Father, in Your Son's name, Jesus, I ask You to bring _____ *(Name the kinds of people Jesus is placing in your hands.)* from the east, the west, the north and the south. Gather them to Yourself, everyone who is called by Your name; those You created for Your glory, those You formed and made, in Jesus' name!

Let them go! In the authority of the name of Jesus, by the redemptive power of His blood and in the power of the Holy Spirit I declare that You cannot hold them back any longer! The weapons of our warfare are divinely powerful for the pulling down of strongholds. Jesus is building His church and your gates cannot prevail against it! Bow your knee now and let them go, in Jesus' name! Let Your Kingdom come! Let Your will be done, Father God!

PRAYING THE PRAYERS OF PAUL

(Using the Prayers of Paul, ask for the ministry of the Holy Spirit to be at work in your life and the lives of those the Lord Jesus has placed in your hands.)

Pray for encounters with God and the spiritual realities of their position in Christ using Ephesians 1:17-19.

> Let Your Kingdom come! Let Your will be done! I ask you, Glorious Father, to give _____ the Spirit of wisdom and revelation so that they may know You better, in Jesus' name. Surprise them with Your presence throughout this day. I pray that the eyes of their hearts may be enlightened in order that they may know the hope to which You have called them, the riches of Your glorious inheritance in them as saints, and Your incomparably great power for them as they believe. In Jesus' name.

Pray for strength in their inner person to know the presence of Jesus and the love of God using Ephesians 3:16-19.

> Let Your Kingdom come! Let Your will be done! I pray, Father God, that out of Your glorious riches You would strengthen _____ with power through Your Spirit in their inner person, so that Christ may dwell in their hearts through faith. I pray that they, being rooted and established in Your love, may have power together with all the saints, to grasp how wide and long and high and deep is the love of Christ, and to know by

experience this love that surpasses knowledge that they may be filled to the measure of all the fullness of You. In Jesus' name.

Pray for guidance and direction to know what to do and how to do it as they complete the work the Lord Jesus has given them to do using Colossians 1:9-12.

Let Your Kingdom come! Let Your will be done! Father God, I ask, in Jesus' name, that the Spirit will fill _____ with the knowledge of Your will in all spiritual wisdom and understanding, so that they may know what to do and how to do it. I ask this in order that they may live lives worthy of the Lord Jesus and may please Him in every way: bearing fruit in every good work, growing in the knowledge of You, being strengthened with all power according to Your glorious might so that they may have great endurance and patience, and joyfully giving thanks to You. In Jesus' name.

KINGDOM PRAYER FOR PROTECTION

(Just as Jesus prayed for the protection of those Father gave Him, so pray for the protection of those the Lord Jesus has given you. The following is a kingdom prayer appropriating the present ministry of Jesus as the Son who sends His angels to war on behalf of the saints.)

1. *He who dwells in the shelter of the Most High will rest in the shadow of the Almighty.*
2. *I will say of the LORD, "He is my refuge and my fortress, my God, in whom I trust."*
3. *Surely he will save you from the fowler's snare and from the deadly pestilence.*
4. *He will cover you with his feathers, and under his wings you will find refuge; his faithfulness will be your shield and rampart.*
5. *You will not fear the terror of night, nor the arrow that flies by day,*

6. *nor the pestilence that stalks in the darkness, nor the plague that destroys at midday.*
7. *A thousand may fall at your side, ten thousand at your right hand, but it will not come near you.*
8. *You will only observe with your eyes and see the punishment of the wicked.*
9. *If you make the Most High your dwelling - even the LORD, who is my refuge*
10. *then no harm will befall you, no disaster will come near your tent.*
11. *For he will command his angels concerning you to guard you in all your ways;*
12. *they will lift you up in their hands, so that you will not strike your foot against a stone.*
13. *You will tread upon the lion and the cobra; you will trample the great lion and the serpent.*
14. *"Because he loves me," says the LORD, "I will rescue him; I will protect him, for he acknowledges my name.*
15. *He will call upon me, and I will answer him; I will be with him in trouble, I will deliver him and honor him.*
16. *With long life will I satisfy him and show him my salvation."*
    Ps 91

Let Your Kingdom come! Let Your will be done! Holy Father, I ask You, in Jesus' name, to protect these You have entrusted to me by the power of Your name, the name You gave Jesus, the LORD of Hosts that they may be one.

Father God, Your Son is the King of Glory, strong and mighty, mighty in battle. He is the King of Glory, the Lord of Hosts. I lift up my head to You, Lord Jesus and I ask You to come and war on behalf of these You have given to me.

Father, let Your Kingdom come! Let Your will be done! I have made You my dwelling, Most High and I ask You, in Jesus' name, to command Your angels concerning _____ *(List those the Lord has entrusted to you)* to guard them in all their ways. I pray that no harm will befall them and no disaster will come near their tents. As they serve You, let them tread upon the lion and the cobra. Let them trample the great lion and the serpent, in Jesus' name.

Because I love You, rescue them from the attacks of the enemy from within the camp. In Jesus' name, protect them and place them in a strong tower out of the reach of the enemy, because I have acknowledged Your name. Be strong and mighty, mighty in this spiritual battle they face. Holy Father, let Your Kingdom come! Let Your will be done and keep them from the evil one, in Jesus' name! Amen.

KINGDOM PRAYERS FOR SANCTIFICATION

(Just as Jesus prayed for the sanctification of those the Father gave Him, so pray for the sanctification of those the Lord Jesus has given you. The following is a kingdom prayer appropriating the present ministry of Jesus as the author and perfecter of faith.)

Let Your Kingdom come! Let Your will be done on earth as it is in Heaven! Holy Father, Your Son is the author and perfecter of faith. I thank You for the hardships of life. I affirm that it is Your love that motivates You in chastening these Jesus has given me. I affirm that You are the Father of lights and that Your purpose in this trial they are experiencing is that they may share in Your holiness and that a harvest of righteousness and peace might be yielded in their lives.

In His life, Your Son sanctified Himself that His followers might be sanctified. He became sanctification on the cross. He learned obedience in the things He suffered and was made perfect through suffering. Through His death they are dead to sin and through Your resurrection they are alive to You so that sin should no longer reign in their bodies. Now, Your Son reigns at Your right hand and He is the author and perfecter of their faith.

Let Your Kingdom come! Let Your will be done! Father God, I pray for the ministry of Your Son as the perfecter of their faith. Protect those You have entrusted to me from the evil one. In the authority of the name of Jesus and by the redemptive power of His blood and in the power of the Holy Spirit, I rebuke every scheme and every work of the evil one to make _____ *(Name your family members, laborers and the people the Lord Jesus is entrusting to you.)* fall short of the grace of God through a bitter spirit, immorality or godlessness. I ask that this hardship of _____ that they are enduring will be of Your Son's hand and His hand alone. In the name of the Lord Jesus, I ask that He will accomplish His purpose in this trial that they may share in Your holiness. I ask that a harvest of righteousness and peace will be yielded in their lives through this hardship. In the name of Jesus, keep them in Your word and as they hear it, read it, study it, memorize it and meditate on it today, sanctify them in the truth!

Holy Father, grant them the grace to look away from everything else unto Jesus the author and perfecter of their faith. I pray that they would look away from this hardship and look to Jesus, in Jesus' name. I pray that they would meditate on the way Jesus endured the suffering of the cross and hardship at the hands of sinful men. Let Your Kingdom come! Let Your will be done! Your Son is the author of their faith. He is the perfecter of their faith. In the name of Jesus, I pray that Jesus would be the perfecter of their faith today! Amen.

KINGDOM PRAYER FOR REDEMPTION

(The following is a kingdom prayer appropriating the present ministry of Jesus as the Lamb of God and the work of His redemptive blood.)

Let Your Kingdom Come! Let Your will be done, Holy Father! I pray for Your mercy on behalf of _____ *(Name the member of your household, yourself and/or the people the Lord Jesus is entrusting to you who are in bondage.)*

I declare that Your Son, the Lord Jesus, is the Lamb of God who takes away the sins of the world! In Your Son we have redemption, the forgiveness of sins. Your Son redeemed us from the curse of the law by becoming a curse for us. He redeemed us in order that the blessing given to Abraham might come to the Gentiles through Christ Jesus, so that by faith we might receive the promise of the Spirit. We have been redeemed from our former way of life handed down to us from our forefathers through the precious blood of the Lamb. With His blood, He purchased men and women for God from every tribe and language and people and nation. He has made us to be kings and priests to serve our God, and to reign with Him on the earth.

Father God, let Your Kingdom come! Let Your will be done! I pray for the redeeming blood of Your Son to bring freedom from the power of sin. In the authority of the name of Jesus and by the redemptive power of His blood and in the power of the Holy Spirit, redeem _____ from his sins. Have mercy, Father God, have mercy! As Moses, Nehemiah and Daniel identified with the sins of their nation and confessed them before you so I confess our sins of _____ and _____ to You, Holy Father. *(Patiently wait for the Holy Spirit to reveal the sin/s.)* Have mercy on us, Father God, have mercy. Wash us and we will be white as snow. Cleanse us and we be like wool *(Wait patiently for a sense of hope from the cleansing of the Lamb).* Thank You for the riches of Your grace. Thank You for the redemption that is in Your Son, heavenly Father.

In the authority of the name of Jesus and by His redeeming blood, redeem _____ from the generational sins of _____ _____ handed down to him from his forefathers. Redeem him from all ground that has been given to the enemy through willful sin and vows that have been made in his life. With deep compassion bring him to Yourself through the Son, Holy Father. With everlasting kindness have compassion on him and redeem him from any and all claims the enemy has on him! Father God, the Lamb died for and has purchased him with His blood for You that he might be a king and priest to serve and reign with Him.

Let Your Kingdom come! Let Your will be done! Father God, by the redeeming power of Your Son's blood, I ask that you empower __ _____ with the promised Holy Spirit to overcome this bondage. In Jesus' name, set him free from the bondage of these sins that have overtaken him so that he may be a king and priest to serve You and reign with You. Father God, have mercy and bring redemption by the blood of the Lamb, in Jesus' name! Let Your Kingdom come! Let Your will be done! Amen.

Notes

Jesus The Sovereign Lord

1. Larry Lea, *Could You Not Tarry For One Hour* (Altamonte Springs, FL: Creation House, 1987) 59

2. Geraldine Taylor, Behind *The Ranges: The Life-changing Story of J.O. Fraser* (Singapore, OMF International Ltd. 1998) 130, 131

Completing The Work Jesus Has Given Us to do

1. Geraldine Taylor, *Behind The Ranges: The Life-changing Story of J.O. Fraser* (Singapore, OMF International Ltd. 1998) 124

2. Geraldine Taylor, *Behind The Ranges: The Life-changing Story of J.O. Fraser* (Singapore, OMF International Ltd. 1998) 132

3. Geraldine Taylor, *Behind The Ranges: The Life-changing Story of J.O. Fraser* (Singapore, OMF International Ltd. 1998) 131

4. Geraldine Taylor, *Behind The Ranges: The Life-changing Story of J.O. Fraser* (Singapore, OMF International Ltd. 1998) 135

5. Geraldine Taylor, *Behind The Ranges: The Life-changing Story of J.O. Fraser* (Singapore, OMF International Ltd. 1998) 180

J.O. Fraser's Pattern of Prayer Applied to the Lord Prayer

1. Larry Lea, *Could You Not Tarry For One Hour* (Altamonte Springs, FL: Creation House, 1987) 59, 60, 63, 64, 69, 73, 74, 75

2. Clyde Hodson, *Coming to a place of Abiding* (Kindle 2013) 27

3. Clyde Hodson, *Coming to a place of Abiding* (Kindle 2013) 62

4. Geraldine Taylor, *Behind The Ranges: The Life-changing Story of J.O. Fraser* (Singapore, OMF International Ltd. 1998) 135

5. Mark I. Bubeck, *Overcoming The Adversary* (Chicago, IL, Moody Press 1984) 38-42

6. Ed Silvoso, *That None Should Perish* (Ventura, CA: Regal Books 1994) 194-197

7. Larry Lea, *Could You Not Tarry For One Hour* (Altamonte Springs, FL: Creation House, 1987) 93

The Authority of the Christian Leaders

1. Norman Grubb, *Rees Howells Intercessor* (Fort Washington, Pennsylvania: Christian Literature Crusade 1952) 84, 85

Daniel Prayer Effort
1. Clyde Hodson, *Prayer Efforts* (Kindle 2013) 24

Yahweh-adonai, The Sovereign LORD
1. Clyde Hodson, *Coming to a place of Abiding* (Kindle 2013) 62

Declaring The Victory Of Christ
1. Mark I. Bubeck, *Overcoming The Adversary* (Chicago, IL, Moody Press 1984) 38-42

Serving Notice To The Powers Of Darkness
1. Ed Silvoso, *That None Should Perish* (Ventura, CA: Regal Books 1994) 194-197

Calling Forth The Harvest
1. 1. Larry Lea, *Could You Not Tarry For One Hour* (Altamonte Springs, FL: Creation House, 1987) 93

ABOUT THE AUTHOR

Clyde was born and grew up in Southern California. He is a graduate of Biola University and Talbot Theological Seminary. He and his wife, Mary Lynne, were married in June 1976. They have three daughters Kara, Lindsay and Meagan, and are thankful for their growing family through marriage and grandchildren.

Mary Lynne and Clyde's youth pastor, Dave Griener, mentored them to love God's word and hear His voice through the word. Dave taught them to study and memorize God's word, as well as, to pray for hours. Clyde has always been given to prayer because of the grounding he received in those early days of faith in Christ. An intercessory gift began to emerge in 1984, as Clyde experienced frustration with the lack of fruitfulness in ministry. Prayer became a part of everything he did. Clyde has watched the Father fulfill His promises to answer prayer over and over again. Clyde has been equipping the Body of Christ to pray and has led a variety of prayer efforts since 1989.

Clyde served in various associate pastoral positions for twenty-five years and sensed God's call to pray for the nations in November of 2000. He was the Director of Prayer Ministries at MentorLink International through 2008 and then launched PrayerMentor ministry, where he serves as the President. Through these ministries he's led prayer efforts and mentored national pastors in 25 nations through 55 international trips.

Clyde mentors pastors, ministry leaders and business owners in prayer, cares for their souls and builds prayer teams around them so that they may fulfill the work Jesus has given to them, thereby glorifying the Father and advancing the Kingdom of God on earth. In 2011, Clyde and Mary Lynne began intentionally discipling international students and praying in the villages of unreached people groups to bring about Disciple Making Movements among the nations.

A Prayer Mentor Booklet Series

Coming to a Place of Abiding

Equipping believers to come to a place of abiding by appropriating the present ministry of Jesus in the heavenly realms through the Yahweh prayers.

God's Calling

Equipping Christian leaders and intercessors to discern God's calling in their lives and assert the authority of their calling as forceful men and women by praying Kingdom prayers through the themes of John.

Persistent Prayer

Equipping the body of Christ to persist in prayer through a variety of prayer efforts in order to fulfill the calling of the Lord Jesus in their lives.

Made in the USA
Columbia, SC
17 June 2021

40445251R00033